A Dog's Dinner

by

Wee Alfie

Other books by Wee Alfie

It's A Dog's Life
Walkie Talkie

Both available on Amazon

More information on Wee Alfie
www.weealfie.com

Copyright

'This book of mouth-watering recipes will make any dog lick it's lips and probably will make you want to lick yours too. But just you get your own feed cos these recipes are only for dogs and boy do we deserve it after all that muck you usually serve up.'

All You Need To Know About Wee Alfie

Wee Alfie is a very special dog who was born in Wexford, in the south of Ireland and now lives somewhere in Northern Ireland, although he isn't quite sure where because he doesn't have a SatNav or a road atlas. He claims to be round about six years of age but that may not be true as poor Wee Alfie can't count up to seven.

He is a cross between a Ruby King Charles, his Mummy's breed, and a Maltese Terrier, like his Daddy, but if you ask Wee Alfie himself, he will tell you something different. He claims that his father was a boxer and his mother was a wrestler, a highly unlikely claim of course and as silly as his previous claim that his father was a Methodist and his mother was a Spiritualist, which he believed made him a Methylated Spirit. Poor Wee Alfie.

Despite the uncertainties Wee Alfie can most certainly talk, and he can talk the hind-legs clean off a donkey which is nice for people who love to hear his stories but not great for the donkey that has to walk around with no back legs.

This collection of recipes and food ideas is Wee Alfie's first attempt at entering the world of cookery and it has taken him a very long time to write. Imagine trying to type without fingers and you will understand his dilemma. Patting a keyboard with a couple of furry paws wasn't easy but he got there in the end and Wee Alfie hopes you find his difficult task worthwhile.

One thing is for sure, Wee Alfie has captured the hearts of so many people, not just in his homeland of Northern Ireland, but all around the world, through his television appearances and videos. He is a Facebook sensation with, literally, hundreds of thousands of followers and he is tail-waggingly delighted that you are one of them.

So how did Wee Alfie manage to learn how to talk? Well, he comes from the magical land of the Leprechaun where anything is possible and quite believable. There are no answers to be given or words to describe such a magical skill, it just happens and that is that.

When not enjoying his newfound fame, Wee Alfie loves to stuff his face, hence this unique book and when he isn't eating he loves to wonder what he is going to have for his dinner later on that night. Then when he's had his dinner he lies in his basket wondering what his breakfast will consist of. How come he is such a small dog?

His favourite dinner comprises of the finest mince followed by a Bonio or a bone. Try to take the bone away from him and you will see a completely different side to him.

'Now just houl on a minute...I don't know what the problem is. You give me a bone or I find one in the garden covered in gutters and then you suddenly decide you want it! I don't think so...I'd love to see how you'd react if I jumped onto the table and wired into YOUR dinner. You'd have some gub on you then wouldn't ya?

There isn't too much more to tell you about your new friend other than the fact he always sleeps on his back and doesn't seem to have any problem breaking wind.

'I think you'll find that most of the time, that would be Daddy but of course he always blames me...Sometimes I think that's why they

have me here. Mummy never does that kind of thing as she's far too sophisticated...she gave me a gravy bone to say that'.

That's enough information and probably too much information, so that is all you need to know.

Wee Alfie, the amazing talking dog, hopes this book makes your tail wag and that you enjoy it as much as he did putting it together.

Introduction

There is nothing Wee Alfie loves more than a tasty dinner, possibly with the exception of two tasty dinners, so this is his very own collection of mouth-watering ideas in one special collection for dog owners like his own Mummy and Daddy. It may well be the first ever cookery book compiled by something with four legs, whilst sitting at a table which incidentally also has four legs.

Many cookery books include recipes from all around the world, but this collection is different as the ideas are invented by Wee Alfie himself or gathered in by him reaching out to his doggie friends from around the country and not too far away from his own house in Northern Ireland, particularly the love of his life, Wee Judy, with whom he has spent many wonderful, romantic evenings, in his dreams. After all, it's very difficult to gather recipes from around the world when you don't have a passport or know any dogs in distant lands.

To many, a dog's dinner involves nothing more than opening a tin of meat or a vegetarian alternative from the supermarket, chucking the contents into a dog bowl and firing it onto the kitchen floor. This book proves that dogs, remember how much they drool over tasty tit bits, should be treated from time to time with far more mouth-watering offerings. It will, without a doubt, bring owner and pet closer together.

So basically, this is a canine collection of all shapes and sizes for dogs of all shapes and sizes, a little more adventurous than dog biscuits of all shapes and sizes.

It is rare for dog's dinners to include a juicy starter but this book helps owners who hadn't even thought of such a thing to give it a go and make that meal on the kitchen floor just a little bit more special. It will have dogs licking their lips and the owners who choose not to create these special meals licking their wounds after their disgruntled dogs have finished with them.

This is the third book by Wee Alfie and by far the most difficult to write as he had to invent or at least sample all the recipes before they were included within these pages. Now bearing in mind that Wee Alfie is not the biggest dog in Europe it took him many weeks of indulgent tummy aches and general fatigue whilst eating so much wonderful food for your benefit. He put on a fair wad of weight, but only on the part of his body that drags along the ground. His ears and tail seemed to have stayed very much the same as before.

'It was a struggle eating all that mostly delicious food but sure somebody had to do it. Mummy says that I should be able to shift the beef with a few weeks of intensive galloping round the park chasing rabbits and squirrels. After the amount of grub Mummy has shoved down her throat this past lock a months, she'd need to do several marathons, instead of eating them that is. She starts slimming every Monday without fail and that lasts for a good couple of days...so I don't think I'll be taking her advice. Wee Judy likes me cuddly anyway'.

Don't forget that a dog's tolerances and tastes are completely different to that of their owners. As an example, you may have noticed that when dog feels a bit dodgy inside it will go into the garden and eat grass. For dog owners it is the absolute opposite, because if they wander into the garden to eat grass it will most certainly make them sick, not better and they would look like right eejits too.

Dogs will eat almost anything you put in front of them regardless of what it is, a bit like school dinners endured by owners when they were little ones themselves. You never knew quite what it was but you were grateful of it just the same. So long as it was hot and didn't move on the plate, you were safe. That is why owners need to be so careful when cooking for their pets, those little friends of yours are trusting you not to serve them stuff that is bad for them to eat, something they cannot check out for themselves, and so you have a great responsibility on your hands. This book is intended to both help you with that and give you a bit of a laugh at the same time.

So here we go then, off on a culinary cruise around Wee Alfie's local area with the occasional trip further afield. It is time to take the boredom away from dog's dinners, rid our four-legged friends of the predictable and let them all enjoy something new. Just imagine having the same food every single night when you sit down for your dinner. What on earth would it be like having exactly the same pudding over and over and over again, yes the excitement of a tasty pudding treat would soon disappear wouldn't it? It must be the same for dogs, that 'here we go again' feeling deep inside. Needless to say if all dogs could talk the same as Wee Alfie then dog owners would have a revolution on their hands and the sale of earplugs would go through the roof. Maybe that's why Wee Alfie has become their spokesdog on the delicate matter of culinary delights.

As a warning to all dog owners, some of the recipes in this collection will seem strange, very strange. You must remember these recipes are not in here to suit you, but more your little pet in need of some new, more unusual treats. You must not read to judge but more to appreciate that Wee Alfie has done his best to please other dogs around the world.

'Now speaking of dog's tolerances, you don't know what it's like putting up with dog-owners who never think about what wee dogs really like, thins to make us happy. We love long walks and big dinners and sometimes we like to be left to sleep a while without having to chase grubby things and putting them in our mouths. We don't ask for a lot.'

A Flea In Your Ear

Before you enjoy attempting some of Wee Alfie's delectable recipes, please be aware that many foods, fine for owners, are not dog friendly. Here is a list, as an inclusive, but not exhaustive one that shows ingredients and foodstuffs that are unsuitable for all dogs in general.

Please steer clear of these or you will deserve a flea in your ear.

'A flea in your ear is not a good thing let me tell ya. Once they're in, the wee divils bed down for the night and you're up till morning scratching your head off. My Daddy does a fair bit of scratching in the mornings, but by the looks of it and where he's scratching, it has nothing whatsoever to do with fleas.'

Bad stuff for dogs

Alcohol, almonds in large amounts, almond flour, avocado, brazil nuts, broccoli, cacao, caffeine, cherries, chives, chocolate, cocoa, corn on the cob, currants, dates, garlic in large quantities, green tomatoes, grapes, grapefruit, lemons, limes, macadamia nuts, milk products unless lactose free, mushrooms, mustard seeds, nutmeg, onions in large quantities, added sweeteners, pecan nuts, pistachio nuts, rhubarb, saffron, salt, shallots, sugar, sultanas, walnuts, yeast dough.

Please also remember that some breeds of dogs are more intolerant of certain foods than others, especially those with gluten or wheat allergies. The above list is a guide but there may be other ingredients that will not suit your pet. Please be careful when cooking along with Wee Alfie as he doesn't want his fellow four-legged mates to suffer tummy aches on his account.

Some dishes that may sound paw-lickingly good for dogs are also out of bounds;

Chocolate Labrador Pie is a no-no as dogs cannot eat chocolate.

Pot Poodles are harmful to dogs, particularly poodles. Hot water will make their fur curl even more, as if it isn't curly enough already.

Waggamuffins contain far too much sugar for a dog's tummy. They make the dog's tail wag but it isn't the healthiest of options.

Curry of any variety is not recommended for dogs as it tends to make them hot under the collar, to say nothing of additional sprints out into the garden.

Yes, it's all a bit of a minefield but always cook with caution and consideration. After all, anything's better than a bone covered in gutters that's been dug up from the garden.

'Those Romans buried a fair amount stuff didn't they just? They didn't just bury bones for their dogs but they also buried each other after they covered one another in bandages. Never

see the point of that one. Why try to mend and bandage someone who's already gone by the wayside. They may have been clever but they didn't get everything right now did they, what ya reckon?'

Good stuff for dogs

Of course, not all foodstuff is dangerous to dogs. There is plenty of nutritious items for your four-legged friend, so do not despair. Here is a guide of food that is acceptable:

Cheese, bananas, strawberries, sardines and all other kinds of fish, beef, turkey, potatoes, cabbage, cucumber, honeydew melon, blackberries, pork, chicken. In fact it's quite an exhaustive list and the items listed above are just the tip of the iceberg. Get cooking and enjoy the experience but please be mindful of recommended foods that will help make for a healthy pet with a wet nose.

Disclaimer

Please note this book is intended to be a fun interpretation of Wee Alfie's thoughts, but he is not a qualified chef or culinary expert.

Because of this we issue a limit of liability and disclaimer of warranty. We have used our best efforts within these pages in preparing this book and the information is provided 'as is'

We make no representation or warranties with respect to the accuracy or completeness of the content of this book and we specifically disclaim any implied warranties of merchantability or fitness for any particular purpose.

All material in this book is provided for your information only and may not be construed as medical or veterinary advice or instruction.

The recipes within are personal opinions of Wee Alfie and they do not replace professional, medical, nutritional or downright sensible human advice.

What the top dog chefs say about

'A Dog's Dinner'

Top chefs from all around the world are praising this book of culinary delights. The following quotes were collected by Wee Alfie himself because, according to him, he knows every one of the chefs personally. The publishers of this book aren't too sure about that, but here are their endorsements anyway.

There is a strong rumour to suggest he has never met any chefs in his whole entire little life and therefore has made these quotes up. It's entirely your call to decide if they are fake or genuine, but if you need help in deciding we would like to suggest that they are definitely fake. Naughty, bold Wee Alfie.

Jamie Colliever

'*A Dog's Dinner* is the amazing naked truth of how a naked chef prepares superb meals for naked dogs. I suggest the writer opens Eat-In Kennels, it worked for me. I would like to add that there doesn't seem to be any mention of school dinners, so I can only assume dogs in Northern Ireland don't go to school.'

Barko Pierre White

'This book is a masterclass of special meals for dogs, particularly for dogs with curly long hair like myself. Well done Wee Alfie, it's a feather in your cap, Ok then, a feather in your collar. I'm off for a pedigree-cure.'

The Furry Bikers

'You would need to travel miles on your Marley Davidsons to find a book so informative for dog-owners. Trouble is, it's killing our own book sales so, Wee Alfie, on your bike.'

Mary Huckleberry

'*A Dog's Dinner* is the perfect recipe for a good meal for our four-legged friends. As presenter of *The Great British Bark Off* I can fully recommend every single page, maybe with the exception of one or two. Actually. Make that three or four to be on the safe side. Do not forget to check out my own book, *The Meals of Mary Buryabone*.'

Delia Sniff

'Cooking is a culture and *A Dog's Dinner* is all about dog culture. If I had a dog I would buy this book. Actually I have two dogs, I just forgot to buy this book.'

Westie Bloomingtail

'This would have been a wonderful book if it had also included how to boil soup in an old Wellington boot or if spaghetti had been wrapped around a dog lead before cooking. By the way, Wee Alfie needs to work on his image and think about wearing silly glasses like mine.'

Nigella Pawson

'I am delighted that *A Dog's Dinner* sold more copies in its first five minutes of publication than my own best-seller *Nigella Bites Your Legs Off* has sold in over twenty years. Having two fine spaniels of my own I fully recommend this book. This book should be made into a television series as quickly as possible.'

Paul Colliewood

'I'm afraid I really don't have the time to admire anything other than myself. I've never heard of Wee Alfie but he seems to have an incontinence problem by the sound of him. Haha, that made me wee myself. I would like to write more but I'm off to have my grey muzzle manicured.'

James Bob Martins

'Love it. If Wee Alfie ever wakes up in time on a Saturday morning then he is welcome to drop in, even though he isn't from Yorkshire and all the best dogs and their owners come from Yorkshire.'

Michel and Lin

'We love Wee Alfie's recipes and if he ever opens his own restaurant it would get top marks from us. By the way, we also do a good line in tyres for your car if you are interested.'

Fanny Haddock

'What in the name of goodness are you asking me for? I'm a fish.'

Contents

STARTERS

Prawn Cockertail
Garlick Bread
Vegetarian Garlick Bread
Fido Pastry
CockerLeakie Soup
Vegetarian CockerLeakie Soup
TerrierPin Soup
Liver Pate
Vegetarian Pate

MAIN COURSES

Yorkie-Shire Pudding
Shepherds Pie
Irish Stew
Lassie-Agne

Kennel Pie
Waldog Salad
Sausage Dog Casserole
Catatouille
Chow Chow Mein
Bark Fin Fillets
Bone In The Hole
Spaghetti Bernese
CollieSlaw
Mutt-On Casserole
Peekalilli
Leprecorn On The Cob
Liverdance
Lamb Muttlets
Quick Dishes
Christmas Dinner
Bubble and Peek

PUDDINGS

Walnut Whippets
Melon Collie
Great Danish Pastry
Pupcorn
Boxer Biscuits

Stick Toffee Pudding
Woofles
Apple Poodle
Fruit Salad
Pavrover

COCKERTAILS

Pina CollieAda
Bloodhound and Sand
Whisker Sour
Bloodhound Mary
Harvey Woolbanger

Starters

Starters are not usually included in a dog meal as your pet, as well you know, is normally straight into the main course with no messing. Dogs never stand on ceremony and admire what has been offered to them so it would be easy to ignore culinary presentation but that's not the case at all. This Wee Alfie recipe book gives you the chance to teach your dog there's more to food than swallowing it whole, running out into the garden and coming back for more.

Most dogs don't have a clue what starters are, but every recipe book includes them and so here they are, a selection of very special starters for the discerning four-legged friend if you so desire. According to Wee Alfie, they will enjoy this new selection of nibbles before they gulp down their main course. We shall see, but the least all dog-owners can do is try to brighten up feeding time for dogs.

A culinary word of advice:

The average dog-eating time of any starter is around ten seconds, so have your main course ready to serve, none of that faffing about sitting at a table for twenty minutes talking about your favourite film as that doesn't interest dogs in the slightest. Just ten seconds and they'll be ready for the big one. So, as starters say, on your marks and get set.

If the idea of a starter doesn't suit you or your dog, although called starters, they can always be eaten as special treats after the main meal, perhaps even throughout the day because, after all, that is how doggie bags came to be.

'I love it when Mummy and Daddy go out for a feed. Not because I'm glad to get rid of them, although it's great to get the oul head showered from time to time, but because they always bring me back a tasty wee treat in a doggie bag. Well it's not really a bag as such but a bit of napkin that one of them has used to wipe their gub with. I really don't mind though even if bits of it are stuck to the food. They think I'm really excited to see them when they get home and they get all emotional, although that could also be the wine. What I'm REALLY excited about is the thought of getting my chops around that big

bit of steak. Imagine my disappointment when they were going through their vegetarian phase. Cauliflower steaks? Wise up and have a titter of wit!'

So, select your favourite starter and have your doggie bag ready to fill later if necessary. Please note, if you try to place soup in such a bag you will make a dreadful mess so it may be better to skip the soup and go for something more chewy if you are aiming for the doggie bag method. Most dogs simply look at soup as a stodgy oul muck and nowhere near as appetising as a good wholesome meal anyway. By all means serve soup on the odd occasion but don't make a meal of it.

So the various starter recipes offered within this book are nothing more than a nice, thoughtful addition to a special meal but it really isn't the norm. A smarter move may be to prepare your own starters for your dinner whilst you are preparing the main course for the dog's meal. That way, everyone's happy and your time has been used admirably.

If you still have the desire to create tasty starters for your dog as opposed to yourself, then here's a mouth-watering selection of Wee Alfie's favourites.

'Ach aye, I've tried them, but to be honest I wasn't overly fussed.'

Prawn Cockertail

What is a prawn? It's a crustacean that lives in the sea. It, strangely has 10 legs but cannot move as fast as Wee Alfie who only has 4. Buster the Bulldog told Wee Alfie he could find them on a chessboard. He couldn't have been more wrong. Buster doesn't know everything, that's for sure.

Dogs love prawns. Well, let's be honest dogs love most things and that's why a list of ingredients dangerous to dogs is included in this book as they're not all that fussy what they throw into their gubs. This is an easy starter to prepare so just follow the instructions and have a glass of wine ready, for you and not your dog, as it will only take five minutes of preparation. No brain cells will be lost when following this recipe.

Just a thought...how do prawns get caught anyway if they have ten legs? They only have themselves to blame in my humble opinion.

Cooking time: 1 minute (RESULT!)
Serves: 1 dog

INGREDIENTS
4 prawns
Lemon juice
Gravy

PREPARATION
Glass bowl shallow enough for a dog to get his whole head in to lick the juice off the bottom
Spoon for mixing
Jug for mixing gravy
Lemon squeezer

COOKING
Take the 4 prawns and wash thoroughly.
Don't forget prawns walk around on the bottom of the sea so you never know what oul rubbish they have tramped in. Don't forget, they don't even wear boots to keep their feet clean.
If you find one of the prawns has been broken on its way from the shop then take to a prawnbrokers immediately.

Put the prawns in the pre-prepared gravy. (Make the gravy by boiling the living daylights out of some oul bones for at least 3 days). Stir the contents.

Before serving, sprinkle a little lemon juice on the prawns that stick out of the gravy for additional flavouring.

Serve on the kitchen floor in a suitable bowl.

The beauty of a Prawn Cockertail is you don't have to mess around with a wine glass, lettuce which dogs find tricky to chew, or 1000 Island Dressing. Just follow the instructions and your dog will be licking its lips in deep gratitude.

Wee Alfie loves this recipe so much because it reminds him of so many wonderful walks along the beaches of Northern Ireland. So it may not be a bad idea to use a water-moisture spray for effect while your dog tucks into this delicacy, but not in excess as they may think it's raining and run for cover, leaving a few prawns uneaten.

Garlick Bread

Garlick Bread is not to be confused with garlic bread as garlic is not good for dogs. This simple stand-alone recipe was created by top French Poodle chef, Francoise Gar. Wee Alfie gained this special recipe by chatting with Francoise, a difficult task as she only barked in French. However it is very easy to prepare and definitely a no-brainer which is not meant to be an insult relating to Francoise Gar's intelligence. International cuisine is a new approach to dog recipes and this is a classic example of how tasty it will be.

Buster the Bulldog once went for a French Poodle and bit her on the leg, so the poor thing ended up in plaster in Paris.

Cooking time: None whatsoever
Serves: 1 dog per slice

INGREDIENTS
French loaf
Gravy (Recipe as before)

PREPARATION
Bread board
Bread knife
Knife for spreading topping
Prepare dog's tongue for licking

If you do not have any of these items you should think seriously about yourself as you're more than a bit of a let-down. Bread can be bought from a bakery and prawns come from a fish shop or supermarket, so it isn't exactly rocket domestic science.

COOKING
Cut the French loaf into convenient slices.
One slice is enough for any dog so there will be plenty left over for your other dinner-party guests.
Spread the gravy evenly over the bread.

Serve with pride as it's something different.

Please note: This is one of the many recipes that include gravy because dogs absolutely love gravy, especially Wee Alfie. They just can't get enough of it. It is enough for a hungry dog to just lick the gravy from the bread and once that has been witnessed you may wish to throw the bread in the bin as they won't be that bothered. Hey, they're dogs not seagulls. Too much bread is not good for dogs with certain intolerances anyway.

This is not a suitable starter to be placed in a doggie bag to be eaten later, as the gravy in just a short space of time, will stick to the paper and the whole thing will look like a right oul muck.
Serve immediately before the main course or don't bother your head.

Wee Alfie would like to thank Francoise Gar for this stunning recipe. It has definitely upgraded his opinion of French Poodles and he's well up for a trip to Paris, all expenses paid of course as he doesn't get any pocket money.

Remember, if you have a French Poodle of your own and you are going to serve them this recipe, be prepared for them to suffer bouts of home-sickness as they roam around dreaming of The Cross-Channel Ferry.

Vegetarian Garlick Bread

Vegetarian Garlick Bread is popular in regions of France where they have a great love for their animals. Francoise Gar, herself a vegetarian of two years standing at the time, created this new dish, to compliment her Garlick Bread recipe, whilst singing the French National Anthem when The Olympic Games were on television. Irrelevant, uninteresting, but a fact just the same. Many dogs are vegetarian but only if their owners are vegetarian too. In France dogs eat very smelly cheeses, but only if their owners also have bad breath. Dental sticks are as popular in France as the Tour de France.

Buster the Bulldog is not vegetarian, he eats anything that's going at great speed.

Cooking time: None as before...RESULT!
Serves: 1 dog per slice

INGREDIENTS
French loaf
Vegetarian Gravy

PREPARATION
Bread board
Bread knife
Knife for spreading topping

COOKING
Vegetarian gravy can be made by mixing celery sticks with carrots before adding 3 bay leaves, a thyme twig and a large portion of lacto-free butter.

Add 2 tablespoons of plain flour and whisk until lumps have disappeared.

Boil for a good 2 days until the veg is cooked, whilst topping up with water every now and again.

Cut the French loaf into convenient slices.

One slice is enough for any dog so there will be plenty left over for your other dinner-party guests.

Spread the gravy over the bread.

Serve with a sense of well-being regarding the saving of all good things on the planet.

Please note: Garlick Bread, vegetarian or otherwise can be kept in a fridge for up to 48 hours.

If you are a professional chef and you intend to charge for this exciting meal, remember if they don't pay you can always call in the bay-leaves.

Fido Pastry

To ease the confusion Fido Pastry is similar, but not exactly the same, as Filo Pastry. Actually, it's exactly the same without the fillings so there isn't really any confusions to be eased. Waste of time and unworthy of mention, but you still need to know how to prepare and serve.

Fido is a Bull-Terrier who Wee Alfie met during a walk in the park. They didn't get on at first as Wee Alfie was scared of Fido, but when he offered Wee Alfie a Fido Pastry this scrummy delicacy carved a beautiful friendship.

The chances of Buster the Bulldog becoming friendly with Fido is simply pie in the sky.

Cooking time: 15 minutes
Serves: I dog with enough to freeze for the following day

INGREDIENTS
8 oz Lacto-free butter
Remember dogs must not eat regular butter
16 oz Plain Flour, nothing with flowers painted on it
2 tablespoons of water
1 carton natural yoghurt

PREPARATION
Rolling pin
Mixing bowl
Wooden spoon
Hand wash before offering to dog

COOKING
Mix flour and lacto-free butter together until a smooth consistency.
Add water slowly until a doughy, even smoother, consistency.
Roll the finished mix.
Add natural yoghurt for additional yummy effect.

Cook in a pre-heated oven at 190 degrees until it's golden retriever brown.

When cool, serve by hand, straight into the welcoming mouth of your dog. Don't worry about a bowl. This recipe is perfect for dog-owners who don't own a dishwasher and need to cut down on the washing-up.

CockerLeakie Soup

A Scottish delicacy popular with Highland Terriers and Lowland Terriers if there are any. This particular soup is very popular with dogs, especially those with dental problems. Dogs having soup is where the term 'Super' comes from, just in case you didn't know, even though it isn't true.

Highland Terriers swear by CockerLeakie soup and so it best to be served out of ear-shot of your children or adults who are sensitive to bad language. Lowland Terriers may well swear by it too, but as nobody has ever seen a Lowland Terrier we can't be a hundred percent sure. Lowlands people must be depressed and Highland people probably drink too much whiskey.

If you wish to take your dog for a walk around Scotland you need to leave by your front door and head north until you reach beautiful lochs and mountains. That is, of course, unless you live in Scotland already because if YOU head north you'll end up in the sea and a cold piece of sea at that.

Buster the Bulldog once went to Scotland to watch the Highland Games and told the big man tossing the caber to go and fetch his own stick. Oh how he laughed...NOT!

Cooking time: 45 minutes
Serves: 4 dogs

INGREDIENTS

1500ml Chicken Stock (Make this by boiling a few chickens for around 3 days. They should be done by then)
10 Asparagus Stems
1 carrot
Handful of peas
Remember not to use leeks in this recipe as they are toxic to dogs. If you have a leek you need to get rid of, call a plumber.

PREPARATION

Knife
Large saucepan
Ladle
Hand blender or whisk
Hand wash

COOKING

Pour the chicken stock into a saucepan and bring to the boil.
Chop asparagus into small chewable sized chunks.

Small amounts of asparagus are fine for dogs but don't over-do it.

Add to stock.

Bring back to the boil then lower the heat and simmer for 30 minutes until the asparagus softens.

Add the chopped carrot.

Add handful of peas, ensuring you have washed your hands thoroughly with the hand-wash.

Remove from heat and smooth the soup using either a hand blender or whisk.

Never stir food with a stick brought in from the garden by your dog as you don't know where it's been. Actually, you do know exactly where it's been, in your garden, but it's still a health hazard just the same so use a spoon or ladle for safety.

Allow to cool before serving as your dog's tongue is more sensitive to temperatures than a human's.

Serve in a bowl with a high rim to ensure less spillage on the floor.

This recipe only goes to show that Scottish dog owners have an awful lot of time on their hands. As a hint it's much easier to go to the shop and buy a tin of plain, simple soup. This brilliantly alternative idea will change the preparation section to nothing more than a dander to the shop and your trusty tin-opener. It will also give Scottish owners more time to go searching for The Loch Ness Monster.

Remember the advice...

Dogs feel ripped-off when given just a bowl of soup, especially working dogs who have been out in the farms and fields all day, and that may well lead to anxiety or panic attacks if they think that is all they are going to get for their dinner. So let them have a smell of the main course before you serve the soup, so they know something far more substantial is on the way.

Wee Alfie was informed by a burly Highland Terrier that CockerLeakie Soup is a highly nutritious meal, so much so that, once upon a time, a Highland Terrier by the name of Hamish ate a bowl of the stuff just before his owner tossed a caber at The Highland Games. So energised and pumped up by the soup it ran after the caber and brought it back to his owner. How is that Loch Ness Monster doing anyway? It must be nearly two hundred years old by now.

Vegetarian CockerLeakie Soup

Another Scottish delicacy, similar to the previous recipe, popular with dogs who can't be bothered to chase animals or consider it an act of violence upon their fellow creatures. Wee Alfie reckons there's nothing wrong with being vegetarian unless there's a few tasty gravy bones thrown in there for good measure.

This particular recipe does not suit Buster the Bulldog as he loves to chase after a cocker spaniel, whether it is leaking or not. Buster is a naughty fella and so he has far less treats than Wee Alfie so slap it up him. He prefers a bit of an oul fight than a good meal.

'I'll take him on any day if the winner gets a juicy gravy bone. I wonder what I'd get if I came second...would be worth a beatin for even half a one.'

Cooking time: 45 minutes
Serves: 4 dogs

INGREDIENTS
1500ml strained Brussels sprouts juice
10 Asparagus Stems
1 carrot
2 strained tomatoes
Remember not to use leeks in this recipe as they are toxic for dogs
Kilt if you happen to have one.

PREPARATION
Knife
Large saucepan
Ladle
Hand blender or whisk

COOKING
Pour the strained vegetable juice into a saucepan and bring to the boil.
Chop asparagus into small chunks, add to the vegetable juice.
Small amounts of asparagus are fine for dogs but don't over-do it, the same recommendation as CockerLeakie Soup.

Add the juice of two squeezed tomatoes.
Bring back to the boil then lower the heat and simmer for 30 minutes until the asparagus softens.
Add the chopped carrot.
Remove from heat and smooth the soup using either a hand blender or whisk.
Never stir food with anything other than something sensible. Rolled-up newspapers, orange lollies and uncooked spaghetti are all a complete waste of time. Read how the professionals do it.

'There are Highland Terriers, Highland Sheep, Highland Cattle and Highland Shortbread. So what in the name of goodness do they do in The Lowlands. If there's no sheep, cows or shortbread in The Lowlands what on earth do they eat? I wonder if The Lowlands are where dogs like me with short legs live? I've already said that once but it won't leave me head.'

Wee Alfie suggests to any dog living in The Lowlands to move north and enjoy a decent diet and get involved with some Highland Games.

But don't move too far north or you will end up in Iceland with frostbite on your paws.

TerrierPin Soup

A simple recipe that allows you to serve your dog's favourite soup, but a in a shell similar to a terrapin without any actual damage to a terrapin. This recipe is basically the doggy version of turtle soup, a delicacy for humans, a very dangerous recipe for humans as it's the only soup that can break teeth and cause serious damage if you bite on the shell. A tip to all dog owners is make sure that this soup is suitably drained so as there are no crunchy bits hiding in the bowl.

Thomas the Terrier sent this recipe to Wee Alfie from the north coast of Ireland, but unfortunately the envelope was so soggy, with what was left of the bowl of soup inside, that Alfie didn't get to taste the contents, but he's sure your own attempt will be just delicious.

Cooking time: 5 minutes
Serves: 1 dog

INGREDIENTS

Soup of the day.

Anything other than a terrapin because they are such lovely creatures

Every dog has its day and this is a chance to serve their favourite flavour with a bit of a difference to say nothing of a completely irrelevant title

A few blades of grass for garnish

PREPARATION

Scallop shell from gift shop or direct from the beach. After all, there is nothing like the smell of the sea

Saucepan

Ladle

Dog bowl

COOKING

Empty tin of soup into saucepan and bring to the boil.

Stir for 5 minutes.

Pour into shell.

Sprinkle the grass garnish on top, an ideal way of getting rid of a few grass cuttings.

Serve to dog with wagging tail, the dog's wagging tail and not yours!

Please note that the shell will move around on the floor so either place it in the dog bowl or on the floor with a tea-towel underneath it.

Liver Pate

There's nothing a dog likes more than a liver pate starter, except of course a lovely long walk by a river, chasing a cat or wiring into a great big juicy butcher's bone. In fact, there are many things they like more than liver pate, but it's included anyway because it's a Wee Alfie favourite. You serve this meal by hand so be warned, you may lose a finger if you're not careful as dogs go clean mad for this.

Buster the Bulldog couldn't even lip liver. He hates the stuff and it makes him boke, but he just loves bacon. Come to think of it, Buster The Bulldog hates mostly everything.

Cooking time: 2 minutes
Serves: 1 dog per slice or 2 slices for greedy dogs or breeds much bigger than Wee Alfie

INGREDIENTS
8 oz Liver
Slices of bread

PREPARATION
Frying pan
Toaster
Knife for spreading
Hand wash for serving by hand

COOKING
Remove lump of liver from paper wrapped by the butcher.

Fry in olive oil for 3 minutes, the liver of course and not the butcher.

If you are interested you can boil an egg in water at exactly the same time. Irrelevant to this recipe but an interesting and time-saving thought as eggs are safe for dogs to eat.

Put liver in a blender and blitz until it is in mush.

Place bread in toaster.

Wait for bread to turn into toast, usually between 1 and 2 minutes.
Remove from toaster.
Spread liver mush evenly on the toast.
Serve by hand after washing with hand wash.

So what exactly is pate?
It was originally a traditional dish for humans made by mixing various meats with spices and red wine. Of course, these ingredients are not suitable for dogs which is why Wee Alfie included this wonderful new recipe with dog friendly ingredients.

Vegetarian Pate

Vegetarian Pate is the more usual pate without meat additives. Fish is a fine substitute for meat and all dogs love fish, even dogfish. You serve this meal by hand, as you do with meat pate so be warned, you may still lose a finger if you're not careful as dogs just love this tasty alternative.

Buster the Bulldog chewed on a finger once, but thankfully it was a fish finger so no real harm was done, although he did say he'd never seen fingers on a fish before. Fair point.

Cooking time: 2 minutes
Serves: 1 dog per slice or 2 slices for greedy dogs or breeds much bigger than Wee Alfie.

INGREDIENTS
Fish
Slices of bread

PREPARATION
Frying pan
Toaster
Knife for spreading
Hand wash for serving by hand

COOKING
Remove the unwanted parts of the fish, especially the bones.
Fry in a little olive oil for 3 minutes.
If you are interested you can still boil an egg in water at exactly the same time as preparing Vegetarian Pate, equally irrelevant to this different recipe but still an interesting and time-saving thought as eggs are safe for dogs to eat.
Place fish in the blender and blitz as before into mush.
Place bread in toaster.

Wait for bread to turn into toast, usually between 1 and 2 minutes.
Remove from toaster.
Spread fish evenly on toast.
Serve by hand after washing them with hand wash.

Main Courses

And so we now come to the far more delicious, mouth watering main courses. The real big and proper stuff as dogs like to call them.

Starters are fine as special treats for your pet but this is the section that is far more interesting to them. Dogs love, and indeed earn the right to a good wholesome meal by way of a thank you from their owners for giving such loyalty and friendship. They will do anything their owners ask if they are fed properly in return, within good reason.

They will go and fetch grubby oul balls, or sticks with undesirable stuff on and they will even jump into a lake or river before doggie-paddling their way back to safety, just to bring pleasure to their owners who would never think of doing the same thing on a freezing cold day. For that they deserve all the rewards that are going, and a good main course meal has to be top of the list. Starters, yes. Pudding yes too, but the main course is what it is all about.

Don't forget to keep an eye on unfriendly ingredients as although dogs will eat anything that doesn't mean that anything and everything is good for their delicate stomachs.

Yorkie-Shire Pudding

Yorkshire Puddings that are eaten by dog-owners in Yorkshire are round in shape because the original recipe was invented by an Airedale Terrier who lived in Yorkshire and created the original Yorkie-Shire Pudding in his dog bowl. Perhaps more interestingly he was also round in shape himself.

Yorkie-Shire puddings are big things, as indeed are Airedale Terriers, they being the reason that Yorkie-Shire Puddings are big things too. All a bit Irish but it makes sense to Wee Alfie. If you are interested, the difference between a human's Yorkshire pudding and a Lancashire hot-pot is about twenty miles. Gloucestershire cheese is a bit further away.

Cooking time: approx. 20 minutes
Serves: 2 normal dogs or 1 St. Bernard

Before we go any further this recipe is based on the Yorkshire tradition of it being a complete meal in itself and not an addition to a roast dinner.

INGREDIENTS
140 g of Plain flour
200 ml Lacto-free milk
4 eggs
Gravy
Cooking oil

PREPARATION
Mixing bowl
Baking tin
Whisk
Sift

COOKING
Pre-heat oven to 200c.
Pre-heat cooking oil in tin.
Sift flour into bowl.
Whisk eggs and add.

Slowly whisk Lacto-free milk into mixture.
Add to heated baking tin.
Cook until risen and golden retriever brown.

When cooking is complete pour yummy gravy into the pudding and prepare for a mess on the kitchen floor as sloppy tongues get to work.

Shepherds Pie

This particular recipe was invented by a sheepdog in Co Antrim by the name of Sean, when he realised there was far more to a Shepherds Pie than covering his master in pastry and eating him. This is, therefore a life-saving recipe for both dogs and their owners if they happen to live in the country and work on farms. For those of you who don't know, shepherds look after sheep, cowmen look after cows and plumbers, according to Wee Alfie, look after plums.

Cooking time: around 45 minutes
Serves: 2 dogs - perfect for a doggy date

INGREDIENTS
Coconut oil for frying
500g of lamb mince
2 medium carrots
A handful of peas, the number of peas varies depending upon the size of your hand.
2 large spuds, and we are talking potatoes here and not holes in your socks.
Gravy bones for extra crunch

Remember not to use onions in this recipe as they will make your dog poorly.

PREPARATION
Frying pan
Saucepan
Potato peeler.
Oven safe dog bowl
Sharp knife
Wooden spoon
Potato masher or smasher, or whatever it's called

COOKING

Preheat the oven to 160'C / Gas Mark 3

Peel potatoes and fire them into the pan, bring to the boil.

Once boiled mash them to a creamy mush.

Please note: do not add butter to this mash as it is an intolerance for dogs.

Thinly slice carrots.

Place mince in the pan and fry until as brown as a Labrador.

Add carrots to the mince and leave on a low heat until they are soft.

Add the handful of peas, remember to let go or you will burn your hand.

Place the ingredients into the dog bowl and spoon the mashed potato on top, spreading over evenly.

Garnish with crushed gravy bones and a few bits of grass from the garden and heat until potato is lightly golden, as golden as a Retriever but hopefully not as hairy.

Leave to cool for a bit while your dog drools all over the kitchen floor.

Serve to your pet and wait for the letter of thanks from a nearby shepherd. If there are no shepherds nearby to where you live then go online. Don't email a shepherd because they get up really early in the morning and go to bed early too so, quite honestly, they have better things to do than muck around on a computer.

Irish Stew

Being born in Wexford, Southern Ireland, Wee Alfie has to include Irish Stew in this recipe book, but the ingredients are not essential.

Basically this recipe is nothing more than leftovers from a dog-owner's dinner as they always cook more than they can eat, their eyes being bigger than their bellies. Hence loads of leftovers for their pets. So this not so much a recipe but more a few useful tips for dogs and how to get their paws on Irish Stew.

Cooking time: Irrelevant as it has already been cooked.
Serves: 1 dog as there probably won't be enough leftovers to share.

METHOD
Sit nicely while owner finishes dinner.
Follow owner into kitchen and wait patiently.
As owner approaches the pedal-bin rattle dog-bowl with paw.
Wag tail and cock head lovingly to one side to obtain cuteness overload.

Whine very slightly as owners picks up dog-bowl.

Sit.

Job done.

When Irish Stew was first invented in Ireland the ingredients included things called mutton chops. But many years have passed since then and Irish Stew can now be eaten in loads of other countries. However, it is disrespectful to its Irish traditional recipe to call it English, Scottish, Welsh or even Swedish Stew. Respect must be maintained at all times. However, for further clarification, the Welsh eat rarebits, the Scottish eat haggis and the English spend all their time trying to beat the Irish at rugby instead of cooking. Enough said.

'Some people ask me is Irish Stew good for dogs and does it help them grow up to be big and strong? Wadda you think? Have you ever seen the size of an Irish Wolfhound? It's the tallest dog in the whole wide world and that came about from it being brought up on Irish Stew. That's answered that question anyway.'

WARNING:

If your dog is reaching the size of an Irish Wolfhound you are giving it too much Irish Stew and should revert to slimming biscuits immediately. If you are the same size as an Irish Wolfhound you are too small and get in touch with Snow White.

Lassie-Agne

This is the perfect meal for dogs about to set off to rescue children trapped down mine-shafts or stranded on a block of ice surrounded by hungry polar bears. In a nutshell, this recipe could be an absolute life-saver.

This recipe first appeared many years ago and is a tribute to a former film star, not John Whine or Clint Beastwood, but a Rough Collie known as Lassie. She first appeared in 1943 in a film called Lassie Come Home, so she is now over 80 years old, or 560 in dog years so she's probably having joint problems in her back legs by now and a few 'wee' accidents in the kitchen at night.

Cooking time: 40 minutes
Serves: 6 dogs or can be frozen to serve 1 dog 6 times.

INGREDIENTS
600g beef mince
Chopped tomatoes
Tomato puree
Basil
PLEASE NOTE: Dogs cannot eat green tomatoes or onions
Carrots
White sauce made with Lacto-free butter, 140g plain white flour, 200ml lacto-free milk, 50g cheese.
Lasagne sheets

PREPARATION
Large frying pan
Low dish for oven
Saucepan
Spoon
Whisk

COOKING
Fry mince until brown and add tomatoes.

Add basil and tomato puree into mix.
Simmer on low heat.
Add finely chopped carrots.

To make Lassie-Agne sauce:
Melt lacto-free butter in saucepan on a low heat.
Add flour and stir into a paste.
Whisk in milk until sauce consistency and cook for a few minutes.
Add cheese and allow to melt.

Line dish with layer of mince mixture.
Lay lasagne sheets on top.
Spread thin layer of white sauce.
Continue and build layers.
Cook at 175C for 40 minutes.

WARNING: Adding ridiculous numbers of layers could be a threat to low-flying aircraft so do not make this recipe near an airfield.

Kennel Pie

The difference between Kennel Pie, the dog equivalent of Cottage Pie, is that Kennel Pie is made with beef and the other is made with lamb. Therefore, Kennel Pie is definitely a much more popular choice with sheep as well as dogs.

You may also have noticed that kennels are an awful lot smaller than cottages and that makes them an ideal one-meal recipe for a dog. However, if you choose to freeze what's left they should perhaps be served as Igloo Pie, but remember your dog is not a husky, unless it has a sore throat.

Cooking time: 40 minutes
Serves: 2 dogs

INGREDIENTS
Beef mince
Potatoes
Peas
Carrots
Gravy

PREPARATION
Frying pan
Saucepan
Oven safe dog bowl
Sharp knife
Wooden spoon
Potato masher or smasher, or whatever you call it.

COOKING
Preheat the oven to 160C / Gas Mark 3
Peel potatoes place them in pan, bring to boil.
Once boiled mash them to a creamy mush.
PLEASE NOTE: Do not add butter to this mash as it is an intolerance for dogs.
Thinly slice carrots.

Place beef mince in the pan and fry until brown.
Add carrots to the mince and leave on a low
heat until they are soft.
Add the handful of peas, remember to let go or
you will burn your hand.
Add carrots.
Place the ingredients into the dog bowl and
spoon the mashed potato on top, spreading
over evenly.
Garnish with crushed gravy bones and cook in
the oven until potato is lightly golden.
Allow to cool at the absolute dismay of your
pooch.

Serve to your pet and wait for the letter of
thanks from previously worried sheep.

Waldog Salad

There is nothing better on a beautiful summer's evening than sitting out in the garden enjoying a refreshing salad. Aye right, try telling that to your dog and you won't be getting a faithful nod of agreement. A much better way of spending a beautiful summer's evening is to be running through the woods or splashing in the water chasing a stick, *(that's the dog, not you)* but your dog must be grateful for small mercies.

Salads are not their favourite meals by any means and so you need to make them far more interesting with the limited ingredients dogs are allowed to eat. Waldog Salad is one such recipe they just may not turn their wet noses up at. Sure just give it a try.

Cooking time: Zero and thus a result

Serves: A few dogs if you have a decent vegetable garden.

INGREDIENTS

2 carrots

2 tomatoes, ensuring they are not green, a danger to dogs

Pea pods

Sweetcorn, but not corn on the cob

Cucumber

Cabbage

Dressing (Mini bones for dogs, blended in a little water)

PREPARATION

Salad bowl

Sharp knife

Salad spoon

Biscuit cruncher

COOKING

Don't be ridiculous, this is a salad and if you feel you need help when cooking a salad it is advisable you seek professional help.

Either that or you drink too much. Failing that, just go and buy a tin of dog food from the supermarket, sit down and have a wee read of one of Wee Alfie's other books.

Sausage Dog Casserole

This is not so much a recipe but more a method of cooking that will benefit dogs that are vertically challenged.

They say every dog has its day and for short dogs to have their days too, then meals must be presented in a way that allows total enjoyment and within reach of their slabbering tongues.

When preparing a Sausage Dog Casserole please remember that the method of presentation is in the title.

The fear of any Sausage Dog, particularly a hungry Sausage Dog, is that they can become frustrated if they cannot reach their food due to a high-rimmed dog bowl, causing them to start nibbling at their owns claws and paws.

So remember, nice big meals are all very well for dogs but do serve with width in mind as opposed to height.

Catatouille

This is a recipe inspired by a dish of a similar name, Ratatouille from France, where French Poodles come from. It's common knowledge that most dogs can't stand the sight of a cat, but they dislike rats even more so this is a nice alternative.

This is a recipe that is far easier to cook than to spell or pronounce unless you just happen to live in France, in which case you maybe should have thought about buying the French language version of this book, which would have been a complete waste of time as it doesn't exist.

Cooking time: 30 minutes
Serves: 1 dog with enough to freeze for another meal.

INGREDIENTS
4 Tomatoes, definitely not green tomatoes
2 Courgettes
Tablespoon of Olive oil
Gravy, loads of yummy gravy
PLEASE NOTE: Do not add mushrooms or onions as these are dangerous ingredients for dogs.

PREPARATION
Wok
Wooden spoon
Knife
Jug for gravy

COOKING
Add Olive Oil to wok and bring to heat.
Slice the tomatoes and courgettes and place them in the oil.
Stir until it becomes a red and green mess.
Add gravy.
Serve on kitchen floor to the absolute horror of your owners.

Chow Chow Mein

Chow Chow Mein is a Chinese dish consisting of stir-fried noodles, not to be confused with stir-fried Poodles, something that shouldn't even be considered no matter how much they misbehave. It is essentially a take-out meal for your dog, but why not stay at home and prepare it yourself?

Please note: Chinese noodles are not recommended for dogs due to high salt content, so this recipe uses rice noddles. Any pasta dish is fine for a dog unless it has gluten or wheat allergies so be careful.

Cooking time: 20 minutes
Serves: 2 dogs

INGREDIENTS
225g Rice Noodles
2 tablespoons of sesame oil
100g boneless cooked and shredded chicken breasts
Vegetables to suit your dog's favourites (if they have any)
Gravy
Maybe more gravy, you can never give a dog too much gravy
Do not add Soy Sauce or garlic cloves as they are harmful to dogs, as are nasty much bigger dogs with sharp teeth, just so as you know

PREPARATION
Mixing bowls and wooden spoons, have a few at hand
Pan
Frying pan or wok
Gravy boat
Mop for the floor

COOKING

Boil the rice noodles in water for 3 minutes.

Let the noodles drain and add the sesame oil.

Add shredded chicken breasts.

Stir fry for 2 minutes.

Add gravy.

The mixture is complete.

Serve in two bowls (if you have 2 dogs that is) and be prepared for spillage on the floor.

Bark Fin Fillets

This dish may well sound similar to Shark Fin Soup but don't be fooled. It's a simple fish dish consisting of a fish much easier to catch than a shark covered in yummy gravy. Sharks are always ragin at the best of times but even more so if they think they're about to lose a fin, so best to not even think about it. It's a quick recipe to prepare and an even quicker one to eat.

Lots of dog-slurping will occur so best not to serve whilst watching your favourite television programme.

A recipe dedicated to Fergal Sharkey.

Cooking time: 15 minutes
Serves: 1 dog

INGREDIENTS
Fish fillet
Gravy
Lacto-free butter
Coconut oil

PREPARATION
Enamel dish
Jug

COOKING
Fillet the fish and if you have caught the fish yourself remember to remove the hook.
Heat coconut oil in enamel dish on the hob.
Add fish and spread lacto-free butter lightly on top.
Allow to simmer on low heat for 10 minutes.
Add Gravy to result.
Serve with pride.

The big question is which fish to use and the simple answer as far as dog meal is concerned is basically any fish that will fit in your enamel dish. So don't be too optimistic or downright stupid by trying this with a whale or a shark, and definitely not a dolphin because they are beautiful, friendly creatures who will jump out of the dish when you are not looking. Oh come to think of it, Dolphins aren't fish and neither are Whales, so we're ok then.

Bone In The Hole

This recipe is the doggie equivalent of Toad In The Hole but a far friendlier recipe as no toads are damaged during the cooking process.

To be honest though there is more chance of finding a bone in a hole than a toad anyway. They live near lakes and jump around on lily-pads, whereas dogs bury bones in holes. So maybe this recipe WAS the original and then stolen by toads.

Naughty amphibians, the wee divils!

Cooking time: 20 minutes
Serves: 1 hungry dog

INGREDIENTS
140 g of Plain flour
200 ml Lacto-free milk
4 eggs
Gravy bones
Dog biscuits
Coconut cooking oil

PREPARATION
Mixing bowl
Baking tin
Whisk
Sieve

COOKING
Pre-heat oven to 200 C.
Pre-heat coconut cooking oil in a baking tin.
Sift flour into bowl.
Whisk eggs and add.
Slowly whisk Lacto-free milk into mixture.
Add to baking tin.
Add a selection of gravy bones and a sprinkling of dog biscuits in the centre.

Cook until golden retriever brown.
Allow to cool before serving.

Serve in a bowl with a high rim.
Allow for a messy floor so lay down newspaper or something more upper-class like a glossy magazine that sells yachts or country mansions.

Spaghetti Bernese

Bernese Mountain Dogs come from The Swiss Alps. They were introduced to Switzerland by The Romans over 2,000 years ago but, unfortunately all those dogs have since died. So, why not cook a delicious Spaghetti Bernese in their memory. After all, it's an Italian dish and the Romans came from Italy.

If you are about to prepare this meal please remember that some cheeses are not suitable for dogs with intolerances so be careful and don't attempt to use wrapped cheese that dogs will find tricky to open with their teeth.

Cooking time: 30 minutes.
Serves: 1 dog with leftovers for the freezer.

INGREDIENTS
8oz Spaghetti
Tin of chopped tomatoes (do not use green tomatoes as they are not dog friendly)
Dog friendly cheese other than Parmesan

PREPARATION
Saucepan
Water jug
Tin opener
Wooden spoon
Cheese grater

COOKING
Boil water in saucepan.
Add spaghetti when boiling.
Boil for 10 minutes.
Add tomatoes and simmer for 15 minutes.

This a simple meal to prepare if you are in a hurry or if you have friends coming round and you need to spend time preparing a nicer meal for yourself.

To make the whole dish far more authentic you could open the tin of tomatoes with a Swiss Army Knife, and you might as well manicure your nails at the same time. WIN WIN!

CollieSlaw

Coleslaw is a tasty side dish for dog owners and it's exactly the same for dogs too. They love the stuff, even if it does look like a squashed stoat.

There are safety measures that must be taken when preparing the doggie equivalent of coleslaw due to the various bits and pieces which are unhealthy for dogs. For instance, cream full fat milk and onions are both a no-no for dogs. So, CollieSlaw is their safe version of our very own Coleslaw but having said that, it's nothing like it in any other way whatsoever. It is especially popular in Wales where most collies come from.

Please note: CollieSlaw is a recipe and not a description of a nasty sore on a dog's mouth.

Cooking time: zero
Serves: 1 dog

INGREDIENTS
2 carrots
Cucumber
Cabbage
Natural yoghurt

PREPARATION
Mixing bowl
Mixing spoon
Sharp knife

COOKING
I said NONE didn't I? PLEASE pay attention.

Slice the carrots and cucumber into thin shreds.
Do the same with cabbage, not using the heart
of the cabbage...yes I couldn't believe it either,
cabbages have hearts.
Add natural yoghurt and mix the contents.
Serve as a side dish with absolutely anything,
possibly with the exception of soup.

Mutt-On Casserole

Casserole dishes are popular with all breeds of dogs but not as popular as the grub that you actually put in the casserole dishes.

This is an opportunity to really impress your four-legged friendly mutt with a delightful recipe they couldn't possibly prepare for themselves, so Brownie points all round. Basically, Mutt-On casserole is not dissimilar to a standard tin of dog food without the tin, so it helps to make them feel that little bit special, even though the alternative is far easier. The only difference is that your home-made Mutt-On Casserole will not contain that horrible jelly muck which can't be a bad thing. Jelly should be for puddings and not main courses.

Cooking time: 1-2 hours
Serves: Loads of dogs

INGREDIENTS
Coconut oil for frying
500g of best Mince
2 Medium Carrots
2 tablespoons of peas
Tin of chopped tomatoes
Gravy bones for extra crunch

Remember, as often stated in these recipes, do not use onions as they will make your dog poorly and you'll be opening the back door more times than usual.

PREPARATION
Frying pan
Saucepan
Oven safe dog bowl
Sharp knife
Wooden spoon

COOKING
Thinly slice carrots.
Place mince in the pan and fry until brown.

Add carrots to the mince and leave on a low heat until they are soft.

Add the handful of peas, remember to let go or you will burn your hand.

Add tin of tomatoes and stir until you are bored.

Garnish with crushed gravy bones on top.

Serve in dog bowl when cooled.

Peekalilli

Peekalilli is the doggie equivalent of piccalilli, a delicious addition to any cold meal in the summer months. Of course, the main problem is dogs cannot eat onions or anything cooked in vinegar and so the ingredients are completely different. In fact, it's a long way to Piccalilli.

There aren't many recipes named after a song, but don't forget to sing your heart out when your dog has finished scoffing. What do you sing then? *Goodbye Peekalilli*, of course. If you don't know that song, try *Bright Eyes, cos everybody loves a rabbit*.

Cooking time: 2 hours
Serves: As many dogs that are invited round

INGREDIENTS
Cauliflower
Apple
When slicing the apples please remember that apple pips are dangerous for dogs. If they swallow one, they'll have a full blown apple tree growing out of their bellies in a couple of years time. On the upside you'll have your own cider supplier
French beans
Apple cider vinegar, safe for dogs
Do **NOT** use standard vinegar as it is acidic

PREPARATION
Saucepan
Wooden spoon
Knife
Measuring jug

COOKING
Slice all the ingredients into small chunks and put into saucepan.
Add Apple cider vinegar.

Bring to the boil and turn heat down to slowly simmer for an hour.

Place in jars to allow contents to be used over a long period of time.

Remember to sterilise the jars before storing the ingredients.

Serve whenever your pet fancies a cold treat and to as many dogs in the neighbourhood that call round to visit.

Leprecorn

On The Cob

Standard Corn on the Cob, a favourite with dog owners who don't have false dentures, is not a healthy meal for dogs. They can only eat very small portions of corn, if any at all.

When Wee Alfie first saw a Corn on the cob he thought it was banana with skin problems, because he had a friend Maurice the Mongrel who had a similar problem. Wee Alfie had never been served such a meal and so it comes as no surprise to any dog owner that he didn't have a clue what Corn on the Cobs actually were. Imagine his surprise when such a recipe was sent in by Patrick the Pug as a suggestion for this recipe book. Wee Alfie read it carefully before realising the recipe had nothing whatsoever to do with corn.

Apparently, according to Wee Alfie's very own interpretation of an Irish folklore legend, a Leprecorn is a magical creature that lives in farmers' fields near small babbling brooks.

According to Wee Alfie they may well be little yellow pixies that get up to mischief and he is currently in the process of trying to capture one to bring to his kitchen, cover it in lacto-free butter and gobble it down helped by hungry dogs, wherever they may be.

At the time of going to print Wee Alfie has had no luck in finding a Leprecorn but as soon as he does he'll let you know how to prepare one for dinner. It promises to be THE most magical of meals on his menu list of other magical recipes.

You may wish to dance around your kitchen table three times in the hope a Leprecorn appears. You just never know do you?

Liverdance

It was way back in 1994, long before Wee Alfie's time, that an Irish composer, Bill Whelan, brought Riverdance to the ears of many countries through an intermission performance at The Eurovision Song Contest. As time motors on, it won't be too long into the future when this theatrical spectacle of dance and music will celebrate its 30th Anniversary.

Somebody suggested to Wee Alfie there should be some kind of recipe to mark the forthcoming celebration of this incredible achievement. Unfortunately Wee Alfie didn't quite get the name right and so he came up with something that has absolutely nothing to do with the original production but a lot to do with Irish dancing.

This recipe also gives Wee Alfie the chance to use a new kitchen utensil and give praise to one of his Granny's favourite groups, The Spatulas.

Buster the Bulldog was moved to dance whilst watching Riverdance on the television but he fell over and injured his paw, a result for all other dogs who wouldn't be chased for a while. That'll learn him to stop acting the lig. He couldn't find a tutu to fit him on the Internet anyway, so it's probably a good job he's given up the dancing.

Cooking time: 5 minutes, a whole lot shorter than Riverdance itself thankfully
Serves: 1 dog

INGREDIENTS
16oz liver
Coconut oil

PREPARATION
Frying pan
Chopping board
Spatula
Spoon
String
Imagination

COOKING
Heat coconut oil in frying pan.
When hot but not smoking or on fire, place liver in frying pan.
After 2 minutes turn liver over cook for 2 further minutes.
Remove liver from frying pan using spatula.
Place liver on cutting board.
When cooled, tie string around liver on edge of one side, but not too tight a knot.

Do not serve in a dish.

When ready to serve the liver must be dangled above your pet, slightly out of reach, until your dog has admirably danced on its back legs as it tries to catch the liver.
Some may consider this a cruel action but no, not in the slightest. Dogs love a bit of craic and playing games, especially when there is a tasty lump of cooked liver at the end of it all as a treat for their trouble.

Lamb Muttlets

Dogs are very fond of lambs. Unfortunately, they are just as fond of them in a dog bowl as they are watching them leaping up and down in a meadow full of Spring flowers. Don't hold that against them though, it's only natural dog instincts.

This recipe is very similar, very, very similar to the traditional lamb chops and boiled potatoes enjoyed by so many doggie owners who are not vegetarian. Luckily for dogs all the ingredients for that good old traditional meal are fine for dogs to eat too, bearing that in mind Wee Alfie had to come up with something new, which he did, and most successfully too.

Cooking time: 1 hour
Serves: 1 dog

INGREDIENTS
2 Lamb cutlets, boned
Coconut oil
3 Potatoes
Peas
Gravy
Mince sauce

PREPARATION
Slow cooker
Frying pan
Saucepan
Small saucepan
Knife

COOKING
Place lamb cutlets into slow cooker for 1 hour.
Remember dogs prefer rare to well done meat.
After 1 hour place them in frying pan with 2 wee
spoonfuls of coconut oil.
Peel 3 potatoes and chop into small chunks.
Place in saucepan and bring to boil.

Boil peas in small saucepan for 8 minutes, maybe 9 if you forget they are there.
Heat up the gravy.

The secret ingredient here is Wee Alfie's very own mince sauce, not to be confused with the humans favourite, mint sauce.
Mix 5g of best mince with ¼ pint of gravy and stir.
Pour the mince sauce over the ingredients.

You may well argue that that's an awful lot of mince and meat, but you're not a dog. You cannot give a dog enough of this delicate mixture and Wee Alfie's mince sauce in his own words are to die for.

Serve in the usual dog bowl but allow for seconds as it will soon be gulped down by your appreciative pet.

Quick Dishes

There are a number of quick dishes for dogs if you are in a hurry, maybe late for work or a hair appointment, that are just as satisfying to your little friend. They will have no idea that you couldn't be bothered to cook them a decent meal with a little more thought and that you in fact put yourself first. Remember, it's all about presentation. Make them sit and wait and they will believe you that something special is on its way, just don't ask them if they like your new 'Do' as you'll give the game away.

A handful of dog biscuits

A handful of say half a dozen should suffice but remember they are not struck on those weird, green coloured ones. Who in the name of goodness would be?

A hot dog

Made from 150g of lamb meat and rolled before cooking lightly in coconut oil. Don't worry about the bread roll, an unnecessary addition to a doggie meal. Do not serve to a sausage dog as it makes them jumpy.

A biscuit from the biscuit tin

Rich tea and digestives are favourable due to lesser sugar content, but definitely no biscuits that contain chocolate. All dog owners love chocolate and dogs would too given half the chance but it's a definite no-no, no matter much they sit up and beg. Sad but true and more for you.

Juicy bone

But definitely not the chicken ones as those bones are extremely dangerous to dogs. Chicken can only be served to dog off the bone.

Absolutely no drum-sticks, but hey, have you ever seen a dog that owns a drum-kit anyway?

Apple cores

Dogs love apple cores and for smaller breeds they are much easier to eat than a whole apple that will roll around the floor as they try to bite into it. If you are going to give your dog such a treat remove the pips as they are poisonous. If you wish to proceed ensure you offer the remains of an eating apple and not a cooker as they are bitter as gall. Granny Smith grows tasty ones apparently, but please be careful with this suggestion as there is no proof that Grannie Smith was a dog lover, so it may well be a trap.

Scraps from the barbecue

Anything burnt to a cinder that's good enough for you is good enough for them. Just make sure there are no hidden bones. Vegetarian dogs are best to not be given such treats. For them, it's better to offer a few vegetables while they listen to chill out music by Paul McCartney.

Veggie treats such as veggie sticks

These can be purchased at any pet shop. They're usually a deep red colour, pretending to be made of forbidden meat.

Dental sticks

Not really a meal but good for dogs and a food that reduces vet's fees so they come highly recommended.

Fish skin crisps

Yes they really do exist and dogs, unlike you, love them. These things are a crispy offering and nothing like you would see on a fish swimming around in the sea.

Vegetarian sausages

Served on Cockertail sticks are another favourite with dogs, but ensure you remove the sticks before throwing the sausage into the air for your dog to catch. Cockertail sticks could cause serious injury to both mouth and eye if you're not careful.

Water

This has to be the most thoughtless and pathetic offering you can give your poor old dog, but they are forever none the wiser. It's more of a necessity than a treat. Before you serve it though, have a wee think perhaps about how you could do better if you put your mind to it. Maybe in a fancy bowl to make them feel more special? Dogs wouldn't be fussed on alcohol, even a dog in a pub would be flaked out on the floor and not hanging about at the bar waiting for a double Irish Whiskey. Dogs will drink water from anywhere; bowls, puddles, garden hoses, sprinklers, rivers etc. However, you may have noticed they never drink seawater. That's because they know better than their owners the dangers of too much salt.

Oh yes, many dogs are far cleverer than some owners give them credit for. On the upside though, drinking lots of water prevents dehydration so is definitely recommended, although very boring indeed.

So that's more or less it as far as maincourses are concerned but we cannot leave this section without giving tips for a lip smackingly delicious Christmas dinner.

Please remember, a dog is not just for Christmas, but equally, Christmas is not just for a dog, so make sure when you are preparing your doggy delight you don't forget to sort yourself and the family out with a nice Christmas dinner too. Remember not to pull crackers near dogs as they can't tolerate stupid jokes and the paper hats would be ripped to flitters.

Christmas Dinner

Well, Christmas dinner absolutely has to be included, even though it's usually pretty much the same as most owner's Christmas Dinner. No fancy title, just a good old Christmas feed for dogs to enjoy on a very special day.

Most of the usual ingredients are safe for dogs to eat apart from stuffing as it is usually full of onions which are poisonous to our little doggie friends. Anyway, a load of humans eating stuffing is more than enough to bear in the late afternoon, after all has been digested. Obviously there is no need to lay out how to cook this once a year meal, so the following ingredients are merely a reminder of what is safe for dogs and the manner in which they should be cooked.

Cooking time: An eternity, usually 4 hours but lazy dog-owners cook overnight and so it depends which category you fall into
Serves: 1 dog

Chill and take your time with this recipe. It's a fabulous way of hiding in the kitchen away from all those grumpy relatives who you only see once a year, much the same as Father Christmas.

'I'm hoping to see Wee Judy this Christmas. She's very special but she'd be even more special if she's bought me a Christmas present. I definitely deserve one cos since I've become a famous author, I have loads of fillies after me, but I only have eyes for my Wee Judy. Mummy says that I can look at the menu but I don't have to eat anything...whatever that means.'

INGREDIENTS
Turkey, but no bones.
Potatoes, cooked in coconut oil.
Brussel Sprouts, nourishment for dogs even though they cause a bit of a stink which owners

have to tolerate. Perfect opportunity also to blame the dog.

Parsnips. Most dogs aren't struck on parsnips. It's all down to personal taste but they are safe to consume.

Gravy, lots of gravy.

Serve in a bowl with tinsel around the rim.

Play Christmas carols on the radio to aid enjoyment.

PREPARATION

2 Saucepans
Roasting tin
Steam cooker
Carving knife
Gravy jug
Dog bowl

COOKING

Peel potatoes and bring to boil in saucepan of water.

Cook turkey as normal but save a portion of turkey breast for your dog.

Add vegetables to second saucepan and boil.

If you're using a steam cooker, allow 15 minutes of cooking.

Carve turkey.
Prepare loads more gravy than usual.
Serve in dog bowl with tinsel around the rim.

WARNING AGAIN: Do NOT add stuffing to this recipe as it contains onion and herbs that may not suit a dog with any kind of intolerance.

So that's the main course done, but don't forget to find space in your dog's belly for Wee Alfie's unique Mince Pies, made with best lamb's mince as opposed to the usual mince meat that dog owners love.

Just cook the mince as usual in the pan and cover in pastry when cool. Bake in the oven until golden retriever brown. Remember not to serve with cream, tempting as it may be. Always give a dog the safe alternative of natural yoghurt.

Bubble and Peek

This recipe is Wee Alfie's version of the Boxing Day favourite of Bubble and Squeak. It was devised when he accidentally ate some that his Daddy had left on his plate on the floor. He was violently sick and boked all over the living-room carpet to the absolute horror of his Mummy. Afterwards he went a bit cold turkey and hence invented this amazing new version called Bubble and Peek, which incidentally is just mainly cold turkey.

The human version is eaten with numerous intolerances such as pickled onions and chutney, but don't even think about giving the same to dogs unless you want to go into the new year with huge vet's bills.

Cooking time: 30 minutes
Serves: 1 dog

INGREDIENTS
Cold Turkey
Potatoes and left overs from the day before
Vegetables...also left overs from the day before
Gravy
Coconut oil

PREPARATION
Frying pan
Spatula

COOKING
Break down left-over potatoes to a mash.
Add coconut oil to frying pan and heat.
When sizzling add the left-over potatoes.
Fry for about 5 minutes and then add the left-over chopped vegetables.
Mix the two ingredients together with the spatula, ensuring the contents do not burn although crispy bits are all a tasty part of Bubble and Peek.
Add turkey pieces left over from the day before.

Please ensure that all bones have been removed as these are dangerous for dogs and although it is tempting, do NOT include stuffing under any circumstances .
Serve after a brisk walk on Boxing Day morning.

Please note, the vegetarian version of this recipe is fried potato with vegetable left-overs mixed in for good measure. A simple dish when dogs are playing with their new toys, or ripping them to shreds which is the norm.

PUDDINGS

Puddings, sweets, afters, call them what you will, are not a normal offering to a dog that has just filled it's stomach with a massive main course. But it's always worth a try in the hope your little pals appreciate the effort you've made to make their lives that wee bit special. You may want to let them out into the garden for a lock of minutes before serving a pudding after a big meal. Better to be safe than soggy.

WARNING: Most puddings involve the addition of sugar and other ingredients like chocolate for example, which are not dog-friendly. Even custard must be made with lacto-free milk due to the intolerances of dogs, particularly those with allergies.

So without cream, custard, chocolate and other pudding ingredients, what in the name of goodness can be offered to a dog as a nice, safe pudding at the end of their meal? It's a fair enough question and this section helps with such a problem.

Once a pudding has been served there is no point offering a dog a cup of coffee and some mints as they would much prefer a bowl of water and some mince as opposed to mints. But as they have already eaten there is not much point including this added treat. We all know dogs only too well and if you offer it they will eat it, so best not to bother.

Walnut Whippets

What a way to start the Puddings section of this book. Now this pudding really isn't anything like its name suggests as dogs cannot eat walnuts, chocolate or some cream and very few dogs would have ever nipped a whippet on the leg to discover its flavour. So, walnut whippets it may well be, but only by name as they have entirely different ingredients to the human treat with a very similar name.

Before we begin, some nuts are a culinary hazard to both dogs and their owners. Keep dogs away from, as another important reminder, cashews, hickory nuts, macadamia nuts, pecans, pistachios and walnuts.

Buster the Bulldog once helped himself to a whole bowl of peanuts that were left on the coffee table by mistake and he went totally buck mad. He ended up running into the garden and swinging from the trees, which only goes to prove that if you give someone peanuts you will only get monkeys.

One final word of advice:

Don't get custard and mustard mixed up. They both sound very similar and they're both yellow, but that's where the similarities end. There would be a definite bolt into the garden if that happened and some chilled loo roll required immediately.

Back to the preparation of Walnut Whippets then...because of how fast whippets can run, this has to go down as the perfect fast food recipe.

Cooking time: zero
Serves: 1 dog who will never share such a treat with others

INGREDIENTS
Unsalted peanuts
Low-fat whipped cream
Banana

PREPARATION
Bowl
Spoon
Sharp knife

COOKING
Empty half a bag of unsalted peanuts into a bowl.
Add low-fat whipped cream and stir.
Slice banana and decorate around edge of dog bowl.
Stand back because they will straight in on this one.

Reminder: If your dog has a lactose intolerance, mix the peanuts with natural yoghurt and play safe.

Melon Collie

This delicious recipe first came to the attention of Wee Alfie through a day dreamer of a Collie colleen by the name of Cara who often felt sorry for herself and thus invented this dish to cheer herself up.

It was a great success as it will be for your dog too. Dogs love fruits and all melons are safe for them to eat but please ensure all pips are removed.

Cooking time: Zero
Serves: 1 Large Dog or two small ones

INGREDIENTS
1 Honeydew melon
6 Strawberries
Carton of natural yoghurt

PREPARATION
Bowl
Knife

COOKING
Slice honeydew melon into cubes to allow for easy digestion.
Cut 6 strawberries in half for the same reason.
Add carton of yoghurt and stir until the whole thing looks desirable to a doggie.
Do not add any additional juice other than that which is naturally in the sliced fruit as some juices contain certain ingredients that may concern a dog with lacto intolerances.
Serve outdoors.

Please note: This recipe is more a special treat than a full meal to fill their tummies. It is particularly welcome on a hot summer's day so never consider this as a substitute for a wholesome Christmas dinner or any other winter grub as your dog will be up in paws if this is all they get.

Wee Alfie would like to thank Cara the Collie for this tasty offering.

Great Danish Pastry

Scandinavia and the people who live there, Scandinavians as they are known, pride themselves in their various pastry recipes, especially those delicately prepared as juicy dog puddings.

This particular recipe was sent in by Wee Alfie's pen pal Olaf, the Great Dane. How great was Olaf? Well, he could write letters and text other dogs and so he has to go down as being officially great.

When preparing this speciality please remember that Great Danes are large dogs who need loads more to eat than one the size of Wee Alfie. When the recipe came through, the measurements were listed as a bucket of this and a bucket of that and so Wee Alfie has adjusted it to suit all dogs of all sizes.

Cooking time: Quite a long process
Serves: 1 large dog or 2 smaller breeds

INGREDIENTS
2 eggs (that's chicken's eggs as ostrich eggs will be far too big)
1 carton of natural yoghurt
100ml water
1 tablespoon lacto-free white flour
Coconut oil

PREPARATION
Whisk
Bowl
Rolling pin

COOKING
Mix the flour, eggs and natural yoghurt in a large bowl and knead for 1 minute.
Place in another bowl brushed with coconut oil.
Cover with cling film and allow mixture to rise for 1 hour.
Using a rolling pin flatten the mixture on a flat surface that has been sprinkled with lacto-free flour.

When rectangular in shape, fold the edges over to suit your own design, allowing 15 minutes chill time with each fold.

Heat oven to 180C/Gas 4 and cook until a golden colour, that's the ingredients and not the oven. The oven can be any colour you wish.

When your Great Danish Pastry has cooked please remember not to add nut pieces on the top. It may be better to sprinkle just a couple of dog biscuits for that special effect.

Serve with Scandinavian satisfaction.

Wee Alfie would like to thank Olaf for this fantastic recipe from a country too far away to see, even from the top of a big hill. Great Danes grow tall in the hope they can be seen from afar but it's all in vain. If you cannot see the giraffes and elephants in Africa with the naked eye then there's no hope of spotting a Great Dane galloping around in Scandinavia, but hey, they mean well and that's all that's important.

If you want to know what they sound like over there then just listen to this selection of ABBA-style doggie songs composed for the dinner table:

The Dinner Takes It All
Chicken Tikka
FurNando
Mummy Mia
Waterpoo-dle
S.O.S (Save our Sausages)
Dancing Queen of Puddings
I Poo, I Poo, I Poo

Pupcorn

Dogs very seldom go to a cinema, if at all, and so Pupcorn is a new recipe for dogs that Wee Alfie came across by chance. Come to think of it, when was a dog ever allowed next to or near a cinema?

There are actually far more dogs in films than dogs that watch films. The same can be said for sharks and dinosaurs.

'There was I in the park, minding my very own business, or more accurately getting rid of my very own stinky business, when I stumbled across an empty bag of popcorn that had been mindlessly thrown away by some great big eejit. The ingredients written on the bag were interesting but not at all suitable for a wee dog like me, so I set about inventing a far more dog-friendly alternative. I've spent hours and hours chewing pupcorn while Mummy and Daddy are trying to watch the latest films on the television and I can't even begin to tell ya how much the loud chewing annoys them. So because of that

and that alone, this recipe comes highly recommended from me. Go for it! They'll be beyond ragin.'

Cooking time: 5 minutes
Be aware that dogs always prefer crunchy to soggy food.
Serves: 2 dogs out on a date

INGREDIENTS
Popping Corn
Coconut oil
Salt substitute like crushed gravy bones
Gravy

PREPARATION
Cooking pot with thin bottom (alternatively use a wok)
Gravy dish

COOKING
Heat coconut oil until bubbling.
Add the pieces of corn and wait, usually 5 to 10 seconds, until they begin to explode.
Do not place the lid on the cooking pot if you want a nice crispy result and it's great craic chasing them around the kitchen when they explode.
Add a tiny pinch of your salt substitute.

When cooked empty contents onto a bowl of delicious gravy. In fact, this dish may well be nothing more than a pathetic excuse to have more gravy.

Serve to the two dogs lying beside the fire reading poetry to one another.

Recommended poets to enhance such a wonderful, literary occasion:

Pam Airedale
Edgar Allan Poodle
Samuel Taylor Collieridge
Alfie Lord Tennyson
John Mealton

Boxer Biscuits

Boxer biscuits are always a special treat for dogs and they are safe to eat in moderation. They come in three varieties, lightweight, middleweight and heavyweight, and you can therefore quickly select the appropriate biscuit to suit the size and greediness of your dog and then you can just get on and do the rounds. Wee Alfie suggests a selection of cheese to complete this tasty, after main-course, snack.

Cheese is a safe food for dogs and just like dogs, cheese comes in many varieties. Ensure you do not use cheese that contains herbs and spices. Recommended types are listed below.

To make the whole experience more authentic, your dog must sit patiently waiting in a corner of the room until you ring a bell. Then it's gloves off time.

'I've always thought it was dead funny that boxer dogs have gubs on them that look

like they've been in an actual boxing fight, although I'd never say that to their face. Not like me though, all well groomed, dickied up and a bit of a looker by all accounts (Mummy and Daddy's words mainly). I reckon they must have met up with Buster the Bulldog at some point for a bit of an oul scrap. Pugs look like they've been in the ring too. My Daddy thinks pugs are things you stick in the wall when your computer dies. Ah well, he has his good points too because he chose me, he's no goats toe.'

Cooking time: zero
Serves: 1 dog

INGREDIENTS
Biscuits
Cheeses
Lacto-free butter

Please note: If your dog has a wheat intolerance then just offer a piece of cheese, it's better than nothing.

PREPARATION
Biscuit tin
Cheese board
Knife
Flat board

COOKING
Absolutely NONE!

Remove biscuits from tin, 3 biscuits are recommended as an ample quantity.
Spread lacto-free butter on biscuits if appropriate for your dog.
Place cheese onto biscuits.

Serve on a flat board that allows your dog to shove the biscuits directly into their gub.

Recommended cheeses
for this delightful delicacy:

Red Setter Leicester
Growlda
Mutterella
Staffordshire Terrier

Stick Toffee Pudding

Be careful with this recipe. It's a favourite of Wee Alfie's but isn't suitable to many dogs. For starters it all depends what sticks you're going to use. Let's assume they are all found when out walking but don't use sticks with thorns on them like bits of hawthorn trees or climbing roses. They may smell nice but they can both rip the throat out of ya.

Please ensure you offer a very small portion of this pudding to your dog as too many dates can cause tummy ache.

Here is a list of no-nos:

Red Hawthorn, Honey locust, Cherry and Maple Plum, Silver Birch and Prickly Pear, some of which are not seen too often in Northern Ireland, but it's worth marking your card anyway.

Cooking time: 1 to 2 hours
Serves: 2 or more dogs with strong tummies

INGREDIENTS
225g dates
200ml water
2 eggs
65g lacto-free butter
175g self-raising flour
Natural yoghurt

PREPARATION
Saucepan
Mixing bowl
Stick

COOKING
Pour boiling water on dates and leave to cool for 30 minutes.

Mix eggs with 2 tablespoons of natural yoghurt and self-raising flour.

Do not add black treacle or bicarbonate of soda under any circumstances.

Add cooled dates to the mixture and cook in a pre-heated oven at 150c until golden retriever brown.

Turn out pudding and place on a wire rack to cool.

Smother top with natural yoghurt. Do not add fresh cream or custard.

Wee Alfie suggests also adding yummy gravy on the top, but that's because he just loves gravy and will eat it with anything and everything. It isn't at all necessary.

Add a stick, not one from the garden but a biscuit shaped like a stick.

Serve to dogs but make sure you have dental sticks at the ready for when they've finished.

Woofles

Wee Alfie loves Woofles. He loves them almost as much as he loves his Mummy and Daddy. Woofles are for dogs with a sweet tooth, but due to the ingredients they show very little resemblance to Waffles.

In other words, they sound similar but that is where the similarities end. Basically, a Woofle is a tasty pudding that makes any dog woof with delight.

Cooking time: 1 hour
Serves: 1 dog

INGREDIENTS
Carton of natural yoghurt
Pineapple chunks
Blackberries
8 oz Lacto-free butter (remember dogs must not eat regular butter)
16 oz Plain Flour
2 tablespoons of water

PREPARATION
Rolling pin
Mixing bowl
Wooden spoon

COOKING
If thinking about preparing this meal, please ensure your dog does not have a wheat intolerance.
Mix flour and lacto-free butter together until a smooth consistency.
Add water slowly until a doughy, even smoother, consistency.
Roll the finished mix.

Cook in a preheated oven at 170c for 15 minutes.

Leave to cool on a wire rack.

Spread natural yoghurt across surface.

Place pineapple chunks and blackberries alternately around the rim of the pudding.

Add dollop of more natural yoghurt in the middle.

Serve to a dog with the slabbers tripping it.

Apple Poodle

The Apple Poodle is a piece of wonderful imagination from Wee Alfie. He loves Poodles as much as most dog lovers and therefore felt he needed to create a pudding in honour of one his special recipe contributors Francoise Gar from Paris who offered her Garlick Bread to be part of this collection.

It's a simple recipe that oozes lots of fun and sophistication.

Cooking time: zero
Serves: 1 dog

INGREDIENTS
4 eating apples
1 carton natural yoghurt
1 pint water
2 pineapple chunks
1 carrot

Yes, it's as simple as that. An apple covered in yoghurt with a few additional bits and pieces, but it's all down to the presentation.

PREPARATION
Saucepan
Semi-circular jelly-mould

COOKING
Bring water to the boil in the saucepan.
Slice the apples, removing the skins.
Boil the apples in the water until they become a mush, similar to mashed spuds.
Allow the consistency to cool.
Place apple into jelly mould and place in fridge.

When cold, add 2 pineapple chunks to represent the ears of a Poodle.

Stick in the carrot to represent the snout.

Cover the entire apple mould with natural yogurt, scuffing with a fork to make it look similar to the fur of a Poodle.

And there you have it.

Serve to the dog and hope it isn't so realistic that the life is scared clean out of it.

Fruit Salad

No fancy names here, just a firm favourite with any dog. More to the point it is safe as you like as dogs can eat most fruit, so long as owners are aware that pips and stones in fruits are dangerous.

Yes, no fancy name and no fancy recipe, just plain and simple fruit salad topped with lashings of natural yoghurt.

You can actually use mostly any fruit you want (definitely no grapes) but here is a list of them that are Wee Alfie's favourites, the ones he would use in his own fruit salad if someone would actually get off the settee and make it for him.

Cooking time: Zero
Serves: 1 Dog

INGREDIENTS
Banana
Strawberries
Blueberries
Blackberries
Peach, with stone removed
Apple with pips removed
Honeydew Melon

PREPARATION
Knife
Chopping board
Dog bowl

COOKING
Just chop up all the chosen fruit, making sure you've removed all pips and stones.
Place in a dog bowl.
Add natural yoghurt and watch your dog lap it up.

Pavrover

Pavrover is a delicious pudding inspired by a dancing dog called Rover who was adored in Russia. However, he had never been to Russia and had never barked in Russian, so why or how he was adored in Russia is anyone's guess.

The Russians have always been very clever at naming places after animals. They saw a bovine creature walking on wet grass and they called the place Mosscow. Then they named another place after birds they heard singing in the trees and it became known as Starlinggrad. When they first heard the Beatles songs they called another place Lennongrad. Some very interesting facts but absolutely nothing to do with this recipe.

Cooking time: approximately 3-4 hours or the time it takes for a nice walk along the beach
Serves: 6-8 Dogs

Warning: Dogs may fight over this so have some bandages ready!

INGREDIENTS
4 Egg Whites
8oz Coconut Sugar
Coconut oil for greasing the bowl
600ml Yoghurt for filling
Strawberries and Bananas for the topping

PREPARATION
Your most suitable large oven safe dog bowl with low sides for baking
An unchewed bone for whisking
Piping bag or old rubber chicken (or other chew toy) with holes bitten in it.

COOKING
Grease the dog bowl with coconut oil, ready for all of the yumminess to be added.

Whisk the egg whites in a human bowl until they're so stiff you can balance your dog's favourite tennis ball on them.

Using the unchewed bone slowly mix in the coconut sugar, this should take the same amount of time as it takes your dog to chase that squirrel up the tree.

Spoon the mixture into a piping bag or your dog's favourite holey chew toy.

Pipe the mixture around the perimeter of the dog bowl.

Shove gently into the oven at 110'C / Gas Mark 0.5.

Bake until crisp and firm.

Fill the centre of the Pavrover with the yoghurt and top with strawberries and bananas.

Decorate with raspberry flavoured dog biscuits.

Cockertails

This is without doubt the most boring section of the book purely because there are very few clever drink ideas available that are safe for dogs. Basically, every cockertail in this recipe book is nothing more than a drink of water with a few interesting additions. A bit boring, yes, but even so, dogs would just love to have some kind of slightly more interesting alternative to drinking plain oul tap water or slurping from puddles when it is raining.

Although it may seem a good idea to give your dog a special drink every so often, it is definitely not recommended. For instance, alcohol may seem like a fun idea (if indeed you are a complete idiot) but all alcohol is toxic for dogs and is a definite no-no.

Water is the best and really the only drink you can give your dog. All dogs need constant access to clean, fresh and preferably cool water. For your dog, drinking water really is the best way to keep them hydrated and healthy and this is especially true during the summer when it gets hotter and stays that way for longer. Drinking water helps your dog cool down. If you're going for long car journeys or days out enjoying the summer sun, we recommend you have sufficient drinking water for your dog with you and some sort of travel bowl so they can have a drink when they need it. While milk is full of healthy nutrients like calcium and protein, it's actually not a good choice for your dog. Most dogs are lactose intolerant, meaning that milk can upset their digestive system and make them feel quite poorly, leaving you with some interesting messes to clean up. Not all dogs will have this reaction straight away, and it can vary from dog to dog how much milk will upset their stomach. The best advice is to err on the side of caution and simply not give them any at all. We don't recommend you give your dog tea, coffee or any other caffeinated drink. Caffeine can be toxic to dogs and even the smallest amount can give them caffeine poisoning. Dogs are much smaller than us and what might seem like a small serving of tea or coffee could be big enough to cause serious health problems.

'So, wind yer neck in and take heed of this good advice…now what about a doggie friendly Cockertail? Don't mind if I do!'

My Mummy and Daddy like cocktails of their own but it sometimes makes them fall over so do not drink cocktails on the edge of a cliff or waiting for a train to roll into the station.'

Pina CollieAda

A tropical cockertail drink which is inspired from the original Pina Colada, from Puerto Rico in a wee village that is nowhere next or near where Wee Alfie lives in Northern Ireland. A perfect, refreshing drink for any dog lazing about in the garden on a beautiful summer's day with the sun splittin the stones. Considering that's something Wee Alfie just loves to do, it is only right and proper to mention it here.

'There's nothing I love more than lying upside down in the garden getting the sun on my belly with Wee Judy by my side. In fairness, after tasting all the recipes in this book, the sun has a lot more belly to warm. Me and Wee Judy love a good oul walk around the garden but if she digs up any of my bones, I'll ate her. What's hers is mine and what's mine's my own. We love running away and hiding from our owners cos it scares the livin daylights out of them and they usually give us a wee treat when we eventually come back.'

Cooking time: Zero
Serves: 1 Dog but you don't want to be drinking on your own so make double the quantity

INGREDIENTS
½ pint of water
2 tablespoons of coconut milk
Pineapple chunks
Coconut milk, according to the ASPCA, is acceptable but only in small measures, so it's recommended here but only in a small quantity enough to create an essence in the water
A small measure of coconut milk is actually good when it comes to fighting viruses and improve your dog's immune system

PREPARATION
Dog Bowl
Dinner plate
Spoon

COOKING
Add coconut milk to water and stir.
Empty into dog bowl.
Place bowl on dinner plate.

Surround the bowl with pineapple chunks on plate.
Serve with sun-glasses and straw hat for effect.

The human equivalent of this doggy delight contains rum. It must be stressed that no alcohol is dog-friendly, even for a St Bernard who is known for carrying rum when finding those who are lost. They paw it out, they don't drink it themselves.

'Rum is only for them salty sea-dogs and not for dogs like me. I can't abide the stuff and neither can Daddy. He says it gives him a blindin headache. Mummy often says she has a headache too but that's for an entirely different reason, something to do with migraines or because she has to listen to Daddy slabberin on and on about his sore head.'

Bloodhound and Sand

This cockertail is inspired by the original Blood and Sand cocktail that was created in honour of a 1920s movie of the same name starring Rudolph Valentino. Needless to say, that means nothing to a dog but it's interesting just the same.

There are other cockertails named after movie stars but Wee Alfie doesn't watch films and so he wouldn't have a clue about suggesting the others.

Cooking time: Big fat zero
Serves: 1 Dog

INGREDIENTS
½ pint of water
6 strawberries
Sliced orange
Natural yoghurt

PREPARATION
Dog bowl
Cockertail shaker

COOKING
Slice the 6 strawberries into halves and ensure the green stems have been removed.
Peel an orange into segments and add to the water with the strawberries.
Shake with cockertail shaker.
Pour into dog bowl.
Add dollop of natural yoghurt in the middle of the bowl.
Serve with the accompaniment of some vintage 1920's jazz for the perfect effect.

Whisker Sour

The original concoction is an American cockertail known as a Whiskey Sour, but once again is not suitable for dogs. They used to be drunk by cowboys, or calves as they should really be called.

Please note, one of its contents, lemon, is not poisonous to dogs but may lead to tummy upsets if digested in large quantities. One slice is ample but be careful when you cut a lemon in front of a dog because they absolutely hate it. It makes them go clean ballistic and they will definitely hold it against you, turning them into bitter lemons.

Whisker Sour can be prepared for all creatures that have whiskers; cats, hamsters, tigers, Grannies and Grandas, to name but a few. Oh yes, and mice, if you happen to make a smaller drink.

Cooking time: None whatsoever
Serves: 2 Dogs or 4 Mice

INGREDIENTS
2 egg whites
½ pint of water
Ensure water is mineral water from a bottle and not puddle water. Lake water can be a hazard too as the last thing a dog wants to drink is a Whisker Sour laced with frogspawn. Boke!
1 lemon to be sliced carefully as stated above
1 strawberry

PREPARATION
Dog Bowl
Water jug
Food mixer
Lemon squeezer
Spoon
Whisk, an apt piece of equipment

COOKING
Mix the 2 egg whites in with the water and keep the yolks for breakfast.
Whisk rigorously until a smooth mixture or use a food blender.

Squeeze a tiny bit of the lemon and add the juice to the mixture.

Stir rigorously once again or whisk.

Pour contents into dog bowl.

Slice strawberry and place on edge of dog bowl for effect but don't under any circumstances decorate with those stupid paper umbrellas or cherries as the pips are dangerous.

Serve to dog on the sun lounger in the garden (that's the dog not you).

Bloodhound Mary

A Bloody Mary is a cockertail that features numerous contents totally unsuitable for dogs, from alcohol, to herbs and spices, including garlic, Worcester sauce and black pepper. Because of this, this particular cockertail bares no resemblance to the original whatsoever but it was the inspiration of this new drink just the same. Dogs must never drink any kind of alcohol or they will become lurchers, despite their original breed.

'The original Bloody Mary drink came about when a dog-owner called Mary cut her finger opening a tin of dog food. Served her right for not serving up fresh mince to her wee doggie. Lazy cow. She'd need to get her finger out and do a bit of proper cookery or she'll be reported to the RSPDD (Royal Society for the Protection of Dog's Dinners) I have no sympathy for her whatsoever.'

Cooking time: *Again, NONE!*
Serves: 1 big Dog or 2 small ones

INGREDIENTS

2 tomatoes (ensure they are red and not green variety)
½ pint of water
1 lemon
1 stick of celery

PREPARATION

Water jug
Dog bowl
Lemon squeezer
Knife and spoon

COOKING

As with all cockertails it is not recommended to add ice to any mixes as it can cause tummy upsets for dogs. Ice is for polar bears to sleep on or for Mary to put on her sore finger but definitely not to drink.

Fill the water jug with ½ pint of bottled spring water.

Chop tomatoes.

Mix tomatoes into the water and stir rigorously if you do not have a blender.

Squeeze a wee bit of the lemon and add 1 tablespoon of its juice into mixture.

Add 6 small segments of celery each about half an inch long.

Stir the complete mixture with vigour and then allow to stand for a while.

Serve to slabbering dog.

Harvey Woolbanger

Wee Alfie had to include this cockertail in this book as it was sent to him by Sean the sheepdog all the way from the Antrim coast in Northern Ireland.

How shearing a sheep and banging its wool against a bowl of water can produce a tasty cockertail is anybody's guess and I'm not too tempted to try it out.

I have a funny feeling that Sean the Sheepdog might be spinnin a bit of a yarn and has probably made this recipe up anyway, so we may go no further with ingredients etc.

Final Reminders

Bad stuff for dogs

Alcohol, almonds in large amounts, almond flour, avocado, brazil nuts, broccoli, cacao, caffeine, cherries, chives, chocolate, cocoa, corn on the cob, currants, dates, garlic in large quantities, green tomatoes, grapes, grapefruit, lemons, limes, macadamia nuts, milk products unless lactose free, mushrooms, mustard seeds, nutmeg, onions in large quantities, added sweeteners, pecan nuts, pistachio nuts, rhubarb, saffron, salt, shallots, sugar, sultanas, walnuts, yeast dough.

Please also remember that some breeds of dogs are more intolerant of certain foods than others, especially those with gluten or wheat allergies. The above list is a guide but there may be other ingredients that will not suit your pet. Please be careful when cooking along with Wee

Alfie as he doesn't want his fellow four-legged mates to suffer tummy aches on his account.

Some dishes that may sound paw-lickingly good for dogs are also out of bounds.

Chocolate Labrador Pie is a no-no as dogs cannot eat chocolate.

Pot Poodles are harmful to dogs, particularly poodles. Hot water will make their fur curl even more, as if it isn't curly enough already.

Waggamuffins contain far too much sugar for a dog's tummy. They make the dog's tail wag but it isn't the healthiest of options.

Curry of any variety is not recommended for dogs as it tends to make them hot under the collar, to say nothing of additional sprints out into the garden.

Yes, it's all a bit of a minefield but always cook with caution and consideration. After all, anything's better than a bone covered in gutters that they've dug up from the garden.

GOOD STUFF FOR DOGS

Of course, not all foodstuff is dangerous to dogs. There is plenty of nutritious items for your four-legged friend, so do not despair. Here is a guide of food that is acceptable:

Cheese, bananas, strawberries, sardines and all other kinds of fish, beef, turkey, potatoes, cabbage, cucumber, honeydew melon, blackberries, pork, chicken. In fact it's quite an exhaustive list and the items listed above are just the tip of the iceberg. Get cooking and enjoy the experience but please be mindful of recommended foods that will help make for a healthy pet with a wet nose.

When serving tasty meals why not play some soothing music that is popular with dogs? They have their very own favourite singers, so check them out and give your dog that extra special treat over dinner.

Here are some of the most popular…

Spaniel by Elton John
Any song by Joe Cocker Spaniel
Someone Like You by Airedale
Wild Rover by The Clancy Brothers
Whisker in the Jar by Thin Lizzy
Puppy Love by The Osmonds
I'm A Retriever by The Monkees
Hotel California by The Beagles
Collie Malone by Janet Dowd
Lurcher by Chas and Dave
White Ladder by David Greyhound
Anything by Michael Bulldog and Alfie Bone

The rest is down to you as you probably know your dog's favourite music.

'To be honest, I'd rather eat in complete silence because I'm sick listening to Mummy and Daddy

wailin at the tops of their voices every waking minute of every day. It would curdle milk. My next project is to develop ear plugs for dog's and a never ending bone. That should keep me busy for a while.

Thank you for buying my recipe book and I hope you enjoyed having a good oul read. Now it's time to get your finger out, roll up them sleeves and get cooking! There's a lot of slabbering dogs waiting patiently for some new and interesting food to get their chops around and YOU are the very blade to make it for them. Good luck and from what I've heard about your cookery skills, you're gonna need it.'

Bonio Appetit and lots of big licks,

Wee Alfie x

Disclaimer Reminder

Please note once again that this book is intended to be a fun interpretation of Wee Alfie's thoughts, but he is not a qualified chef or culinary expert.

Because of this we issue a limit of liability and disclaimer of warranty. We have used our best efforts within these pages in preparing this book and the information is provided 'as is'

We make no representation or warranties with respect to the accuracy or completeness of the content of this book and we specifically disclaim any implied warranties of merchantability or fitness for any particular purpose.

All material in this book is provided for your information only and may not be construed as medical or veterinary advice or instruction.

The recipes within are personal opinions of Wee Alfie and they do not replace professional, medical, nutritional or downright sensible human advice.

Printed in Great Britain
by Amazon